These Words

Patricia Russo

Copyright © 2016 Patricia Russo

All rights reserved.

ISBN: 1541061470
ISBN-13: 978-1541061477

www.ReadTheseWords.com

DEDICATION

I've been broken for a long time, but it wasn't until recently that I broke myself wide open, pushed paused, and chose to heal. I lovingly dedicate this book of healing words to anyone who has ever been broken. May you find light in the darkest places, a light you shine from the inside out, a light that is yours to keep, to touch, to dance and play with, a light to warm yourself first, before sharing it with anyone else.

Contents

Dedication iii
Gratitude xi
Sisters 1
Truth 2
Options 3
Time 4
Floating 5
Tempt Me 6
Words 7
Extra Love 8
Real 9
Good V Evil 10
Scars 11
Sacred Good-Bye 12
Out There 13
What If 14
Your Lid 15
We Ebb 16
Wooden Lace 17
Sad Eyes 18
Your Cup 19
Complicated 20
Talk To Me 21
Blessed Strings 22
Back 23
Essence 24
Love 25
Our Rhythm 26
Extra Moon 27

The Rain Came	28
Indian Summer	29
Cards	30
Temple	31
Samskaras	32
Dear You	33
No Cash On Board	34
Careful	35
Invocation	36
Ancient Times	37
Ego	38
Heartbreak	39
Babe	40
My Heart	41
Movie Set	42
Falling	43
My Favorite Color	44
Buddha	45
Kiss Me	46
Love Comes In Waves	47
I See You	48
Made of Stars	49
Editing Room	50
Young Love	51
On The Table	52
Your Eyes	53
Perched	54
Inside	55
Here	56
I Dance	57
Ego Death	58
My New	59
Your Hand	60

True Love	61
Old Fashion Tears	62
Beauty	63
I Stand Still	64
Stillness	65
Fire On Your Tongue	66
I Feel It All	67
Dragon Wings	68
We Dance	69
Pin Cushion Heart	70
Venice Groove	71
That	72
Mirrors	73
Her Hand	74
Hand	75
Time Isn't Real	76
Sexy Happens	77
You Remembered	78
I Am Here	79
Practice	80
Energy Shift	81
Dream With Care	82
Rusty	83
Hot Hips	84
Arjuna	85
Foreplay	86
Hungry	87
You	88
Warriors	89
Coins	90
Gossamer Kisses	91
Blue Checks	92
Detour	93

Sacred Geometry	94
Beacon	95
Broken Rule	96
Heavy Minutes	97
I Don't Know	98
Martyr	99
I See You	100
Magic In a Jar	101
Story Book Moon	102
Empty	103
Green Light	104
Out Of Bounds	105
Mission Grit	106
11:11	107
Irony	108
Her Glow	109
Ayn Rand Style	110
La Ritournelle	111
Chemistry	112
Sometimes	113
Badass Motherfucker	114
Weaning Myself	115
I Love The Way	116
Love Wins	117
Forever Darkness	118
Sirens	119
Infrared Lens	120
Called to Court	121
Spring Is	122
French	123
Meditation Pool	124
Covered	125
In a Daze	126

Shared Breath	127
Spirits	128
Dust	129
Flushed	130
Painted Gold	131
Toss	132
Sarcelle	133
Last Life	134
Again	135
Balanced Atoms	136
Glass Houses	137
Just Know	138
Pulse	139
Heaven Spot	140
Ripple Effect	141
10 Beads	142
Seduced	143
Parallel Universes	144
Her Hair	145
On Juniper	146
Your Breath	147
Packed	148
Algiz	149
Crash Into Me	150
Ask	151
Somehow	152
Shade	153
Dreaming	154
By The River	155
Fading Pixels	156
Paper House	157
Tears	158
Matrix Style	159

Shredding	160
Sweet Soft Intention	161
Truth Dancers	162
I Notice	163
From The Stars	164
Dear Hell Yes	165
Spiders	166
Sifter	167
Relics	168
Works In Progress	169
Little Red Corvette	170
Up With The Sun	171
My People	172
Hanged Fool	173
Bell	174
Fine Line	175
About The Author	176

GRATITUDE

We are the sum of all of the parts that bring us to this very moment, the good parts and the not so good parts, the happy times and the not so happy times. I'm forever grateful for the path I walk, for each soul I encounter and for the lessons I learn along the way.

This book is my heart in your hands.

SISTERS

There are sisters
who walk among us

Who do not honor the code

Missed magic of sisterhood
is what they get –
and empty adoration
for the object they sell

I wonder what it must feel like
to be so alone

Karma bed made
with each risky tryst

I live for days
far beyond these right now

With kindness and love
and a full magic cup.

TRUTH

Somewhere on this page
lies the truth –
freedom.

Painful syllables
you cannot speak.

The straws you grasp
will take you down

While each little compass
floats to the top

Take hold
to save yourself
or forever be lost

OPTIONS

Options
low-hanging fruit

The easy way out

Like whiskey, but better

Weaning myself
from a familiar place

To sit
here
for now

However long it takes
to undo
the stamp of the past

TIME

I used to think
that time
was a thief
robbing me
of us

Conspiring
with the strange
human condition
that turns lovers
into strangers –
in a second

But she is
an elixir
mixed with magic
and stars
and a moon's worth
of love –
all for me

And my heart
cannot get enough

FLOATING

Floating above
the needles
and stones,
a powerful
reminder
of self and source

I float
and "rewrite my DNA"
with sisterhood
and rose wax

Breathing in
the sweet earth

Memories cover me
like leaves
and wash away –

I am drenched
in pink light

TEMPT ME

Tempt me
with your
sexiness
so that
I can't
see
straight

Promise me
"something different"
as a way out

Help me
feel
like me again –
closed,
abandoned,
alone

Because this
is what
I know

WORDS

Words
used to come
so easily

A common
language –

I cherished

But it's
the
unspoken stuff
I miss
the most

Extra Love

Where does it go,
the extra love?

I still have some left

It's dancing
with anger
for now –
until the music
finally stops

With grief's baton
and time's
tempo,
the dirge
is boss

I'm sitting
this one
out

REAL

Nothing is real
but the you
you make
and love
in every
single
second

Let everything else go

Good V Evil

Sometimes
I feel
like it's
good
versus
evil
light
versus
dark
happy
versus
sad
alone
versus
you

SCARS

Kiss the scars
and thank them
for making you,
you

Hold your heart
with cupped
hands of velvet
and rose

This love affair
of weighted worth
is waiting for you –

It sets the tone
for everything else

Sacred Good-Bye

Put your lists
in a box
with letters
of forgiveness
and promise

A captured
bedside kiss
will burn
with them

On the playa
in the dust –

A sacred good-bye

OUT THERE

Out there
beyond everything
is a place of magic

Where time
doesn't exist

And love is given
freely
courageously
and often

We are baptized
by dust
and live on kindness

Letting go –
it all burns
disappearing
without a trace

Except for the pieces
we each carry
inside of us

What If

What if
you
lost
it
all
in
a
second

Could
you
believe
that
the
loss
was
actually
magic

YOUR LID

Your lid
is a sign
of much more
than
possession

An outward
cry
for an inward
task

I see you
because
I see me

I love you
because
I love me

You too
will become
ferrite
in this
game
of love

WE EBB

We ebb
and flow

We hold hands
and let go

We love
and lose

We kiss
and cry

We are we
until we are not

And then we
pick ourselves up
and
we try again

WOODEN LACE

Sitting
under
the wooden
lace,
we heal
and hurt
cry
sing
craft
with
our hands
nap
meditate
feel – it – all

We gaze
at all
of the offerings
with compassion
and
leave it
all behind –
letting go
it burns
forever

Sad Eyes

I saw it
in his eyes
well before
it ended

A sadness
so deep –

I jumped
right in
without
caution

Looking back
I feel
that moment
and I
would do it again

I jumped,
swam around,
loved a moon's worth
with
reckless abandon

I loved hard
and lost

Your Cup

Fill
your own
cup
daily

So that
when
someone
comes along
and
takes a sip
you will know
that
there is
enough
for
both of you

Complicated

I'm complicated
in a made of
stardust
kind of way

Simple
seems easier
but it's
never been
my way

Moon dusted
velvet
covered
in fur –
a diaphanous
light
waiting
to
warm you

TALK TO ME

Talk to me
with your
sexy ideas
of love
and loss

Cause me
to pause
and take note
of your
casual ways

Seduce me
to believe
in it again

I want it

Blessed Strings

Blessed strings
unite us

A reminder
that we are one

Melodies
we carry
in unison
on our paths

Our Gopa's
light
we follow –
humbly,
as we serve

Bhakti Flow
our language,
spoken
with love

BACK

Back,
she takes me
often

With words
heart
a glimpse

I oblige
but try
not to linger

With was
and wasn't

Instead I play
with
now

ESSENCE

Essence
on the back
of my neck

Boyish eyes
I dive

You are sexy
in my ear

Drinking you
with cupped
hands

Thirsty
never
felt so good

LOVE

I didn't say it to hear it back

I never do

I say it to remind myself
that it's still there

Without expectation
or conjured fairy tale –
without fear or history

Just there,
for the taking

An unconditional gift

Our Rhythm

Our
rhythm
is an
elixir
and I
cannot
get
enough

As
one
we
move –
like
honey

Extra Moon

We got extra moon today
I looked up,
and she wasn't hiding

A full half,
with subtle
tenacity
against the ocean sky

Pinned there
so delicious

By someone
with a grand scheme,
and a To Do List
full of miracles

THE RAIN CAME

The rain came
suddenly
and I let it
carry me
into its
darkness

Until
I realized
it was
little drops
of light
and hope

A baptism –
inviting
my heart
to open
like never
before.

Indian Summer

It's like Indian Summer
a welcome surprise
when you're not looking

Common hearts
meet
and dance
together
to a rhythm
only hurt ones know

CARDS

All of my cards
are on the table –
an open book

Rolled up sleeves
with my heart
in plain sight

If I'm not careful
with it
how can I expect
others to be

Going all in
is risky business,
being all in
is worth the till

TEMPLE

Each of us
has
a temple
inside

Some
open
up
and let
others
in

Some
are
afraid
of
spending
time
there

And others
never
unlock
the doors

SAMSKARAS

Some bruises
you
cannot see

They are deep –
samskaras

I carry them
like
precious trinkets

Each tells
a story
of
where I've been

DEAR YOU

Dear You
in some
far off place

With your smell
of courage
and your
unabashed wit –

Talk to my
heart
with promises
of
bright days
ahead

Show me the way
with
your sexy
hands
and your
beautiful
light

No Cash On Board

We live
in a
"No cash on board"
world

Our connection
safely
in the palm of our hands

At a distance
disconnected
drifting –
until we bump
into
each other

Then we take a look
and
what we see
scares us,
so we run
backwards
until we land
where
we started –
safe again

CAREFUL

Careful what
you manifest
the Universe
is listening
with a "I sure will baby"
and a quick
pace

Soul crushing
options
in your face

Honesty
thick, oozing –
delicious

Now what?

Invocation

Come like the wind
and take my breath
away
and within.

Touch my heart
with every finger
play it like Cupid's
harp

Gentle strings
standing the test
of time
time lost —
and time new

Come to me from
my deepest
place
and show me the way

Ancient Times

Born of
ancient times
rituals
of comfort
and peace

Beads in
my fingers –
"let" and "go"
on my breath

108 times
plus one,
a marker
to
begin again

I roll
the plus one
a little extra
as I
begin again

EGO

We chat
you and I
about the whys
and the why nots

You spend countless
days
holding on to something
that slipped
away suddenly

You linger –
bruised

I take your hand
in mine
and tell you
to let go

Together we walk
with a new map
of a dreamy place

Where we can
dance together
as one

HEARTBREAK

I wanna die
of heartbreak
just like
Chi Ching's
mother

Following
cosmic breadcrumbs,
looking across
a crowded room –

Drishti
in the crosshairs

I want dreamy
and sexy
and butterfly
electricity –
forever

All wrapped up
in one
beautiful package
surrounded
by light
and tied
with
love

BABE

Babe
rolled
off his tongue
so automatically
that it took me
back instantly

To a place
I no longer know
or want to be

I'm miles away
with no "Babe"
there

No pang –
just loss

And a familiar face
I used to love

My Heart

Salt water
on my lips

Aching
in my
deepest
place

Feeling
human –

That's my
heart

Still
on
the mend

Movie Set

Witness —
eyes
wide open

I see it all

Crystal clear
movie set
backdrops
that could
drop and
roll away
instantly

Leaving us
light, energy
love —

To linger
and swirl

To engage
and let go

To start again

To start again

FALLING

Falling
like a pro

I fall –
naturally
it's
second nature

Caution
whispers
and my
heart
takes note

While I
do
what I do

Forward
open
falling

My Favorite Color

My favorite color
is love

The way
the light
welcomes
each day

And the sun
kisses
the horizon
like
an old friend

The sparkles
cast by
the cosmic
couple
on the water
in the
postcard
where I live

A color
you feel
and one
you trust

It's the color
of love

BUDDHA

There's
a Buddha
inside you –
an old soul

You are
far beyond
your years

Eyes
with depth

Heart
with soul

Hands
with history

Talk to me

Kiss Me

Kiss me
deeply
like
new lovers
who
cannot get
enough

Promise me
this
will never
wane

That
our appetites
will
never be
satisfied

And that
all
of the
answers
you are
looking for
can be
found
when
your lips
touch
mine

Love Comes In Waves

Love
comes
in waves
each
with
an energy
all its own

Some
glide in
extending
the still
waters

Some
crash
with mad
passion
and fierce
power

Some
within you
and
some
without you

Crashing
gliding

Crashing
gliding

I See You

I see you
in the stars
and in
sparkles
of light
on the water

I feel you
in the
warm breeze
that helps
my hair
tickle
my face

I know
you dance
and fly
swirl
and swoop

In the land
of love –
up there
in there
over, behind
all around
me

Spirit
essence
light
you
me
us

Made of Stars

Made of stars
and dust
bones
and skin –
this body
for only
a little bit

We return
to the
charge
of light
energy
that keeps
the earth
spinning

Our essence
fuel

Days fleeting
but we
live on

Feel it?

Editing Room

In the editing room
I pause frames
and discard
stills

And even rewind
certain parts
until the film
gives
from wear

I cue music
and select
the cast

I say "Cut!"
and wander
back to
the fireworks

I left you there
I left you there

YOUNG LOVE

Young love
on my tongue
music
in my head

I swim in
a candle's worth
of light

Time matters
not –

We wrap ourselves
in it
teasing
the minutes
the hours
the days
the years

All of it
paused
with
deep kisses

On The Table

On the table
I breathe
leaving
this vessel
behind

Source
takes
my hand

Forks
needles
vibration —
a nose full
of earth
and
sweet rose

A love affair
you say?

Manifesting

Your Eyes

Your eyes
tell the story
of where
you've been

They lock
and dance
with mine

Eager lips
open heart
wanting
to connect

Slow down

PERCHED

Perched
on one hand
is a Universe
of love

Creation
power
divinity
strength –
purpose

Divine purpose
my lover

INSIDE

I go inside
to find
myself

Into the darkness
to find
light

Into the quiet
to find
voice

Into my heart
to find
you

HERE

I've been here before
the Think. Say. Do.
answer
from Her

It's a game
of chicken

I observe
the signs
so clearly
everywhere –
I am

On the edge
of purpose
hairs on end
heart racing
in-love
with the life
below

Jump

Jump, PB

Jump

I DANCE

I dance
to move
the atoms
of
my heart

I dance
to connect
the dots
in the
sky

I dance
to
heal
myself

I dance
to
the beat
of my
own drum

Ego Death

Ego death

I strip away
layers
until I am
naked

Letting go
of past
DNA
to rewrite
rescript
a new
way

Alone
in the light
bathing
in it –
a baptism

I walk
ahead
with
my skin
on fire

MY NEW

My new
and your new
are
worlds apart

A dozen months
will soon
make
their mark

I wear new
from
the inside
out

Whispers
from
my compass
I don't dare
hush

We sit –
and breathe
and chat
I stretch and grow
certain,
so certain
of
the perfect
fit

And grateful
to be
wearing it
alone

Your Hand

I see
your hand
reaching
for mine –
I take it

We dance
a slow
dance
my pace
you honor it

A mattress
spinning on
its axis
just like
John says

No words
just being –
setting fire
to everything
I see

I want you
so bad

There
I just said it

TRUE LOVE

True love
is
watching
love happen
outside of you
in spite
despite –
you
and smiling
from your
deepest
place

I want
how
you look
at her
for
myself

That
or nothing

That
or nothing

Old Fashion Tears

Old Fashion
tears
sweet weed
on my tongue
dammit
no hiding

At the table
with my heart

Sitting beside
void

Sobering
yet
numb –
in a gentle
glass
with a
handmade
cube

Beauty

There is beauty
in grey
the way
the fog
dances
on the
water
and hides
a whole city
with
her dress

I Stand Still

I stand still
so
I can move

We don't stop
often
enough
to listen
and be

We sip
a numbing
distraction
we busy
ourselves
with work

Taunting time

Sit
with you
in stillness –
is there
a rub?

Listen
notice
be

STILLNESS

In stillness
I find movement
breath
heart
electricity
essence

My magic
lies there

In movement
I find stillness
peace
courage
hope –
love

My map
lies there

Be still
so you can
move

Move
to be
still

Fire On Your Tongue

Go ahead
dance
around me
with
fire on your
tongue
and hate
in your heart

I am water
love
light

Light
that knows
no darkness

I am the
magic
you dream of
and can have

If
you take
my hand

I Feel It All

Breathing
into
the corners –
feeling
each one

Filling up
taking in
life
and love

Pausing
in fullness
gratitude

Letting go
divine purpose
out like fire
catching
floating
touching
igniting

Paused again
with
emptiness
void
suspension
contrast

Sacred space
time travel

Finding the
love
in being
human –
slow dancing
with life
on my breath

The Universe
is my partner
and Source
plays
the flute

I feel it all

Dragon Wings

I have Dragon Wings
on the soles
of my feet
and love
in my veins

Tied with
twisted curls
from bottom
to top –
grounded

I breathe in
humility
thick
and rich

It fills
every part
of me
and stays
on my
lips

So that
when I speak
it touches
everyone

WE DANCE

We dance
you and I
with love
on our
breath

Armor off
ticklish parts –
exposed

Goodness
dripping
from
the light
onto us

And time
stands still
for just
a moment

A moment
full of
promise
and
minutes –
fleeting minutes

In the reel
I will
replay
to my heart's
content

Pin Cushion Heart

Pin cushion heart
tips pierce
velvet

You feel
it too –
connected

Soul language

Before time
and
time again

We are
ancient
and new –
ancient
and new

Paused
for now
under the
fig trees

Venice Groove

Venice groove
whiskey breath
red kicks
and fixes

We vibe
to the
sun's time
as
she paints
her canvas
with
sorbet colors

And bathes
cotton candy
lovers
in her
light

Sipping
for tomorrow
and the
next day

And the
next day

My soul
lives here

THAT

Oh that?

That's you
you see
in the mirror
of me

Let me
show you
what I see

It is love

Mirrors

I look at them
and see me
mirrors
hope
love
sisterhood

"You did that"
rolls off
her tongue
in an instant
and I want
to cry
because
she speaks
my language

I am home

One hour
ours
every week
to do
our work

From the inside out

Her Hand

They look
at me
like
I'm magic

And lift
me up
from my
heart's center

Marionette
strings
of love
and light

All of it
controlled by
Her hand

I let go
of
the voices
inside
and trust

HAND

I feel that hand
pushing
pushing at my
cheek
pressing it
against
the plane

The plane
I take
as an
invitation
which
dissolves
as
my light
breaks
through

That hand
has been
kin
and
kindred spirit
too

Pushing
inviting

Outlook
is king –
it saves me

Time Isn't Real

He has eyes
like yours
sleepy
sexy
pulling me
in

And
French
drips
off
his lips

I watch –
she
adores
him

And I
catch
myself
from
falling

I shake
myself
awake

Time
isn't
real

SEXY HAPPENS

Make love
to
my mind
our
bodies
will
follow

Complicated
creatures
opinions
or not
conflict
for
the sake
of push

I think not

Sexy happens
like
the sky
and
the moon

They dance
with
no question
of how
or
why

You Remembered

You remembered —
every word
but mostly
you dive in
to my
headspace
and
swim around
Ben Sherman
style

And I like it

Take the yogi out
you say
and I listen
risk the trust
give to get

So smart
it scares me
sexy

Thank you
Universe

I Am Here

I am here
listen
right side
left side
mama
papa

Body rings
and hot
tongues

Sacred
wounds
stream out
into the darkness
on I-5

You are
okay

Listen

I am right here

PRACTICE

I practice
with soul
intention
from
tips
to toes

Guiding
light
and
energy
with
my
breath

Asana
my
canvas
intuition
my
ink

I move
on
this
world
of a
mat

Stars
above me
in me
earth
below me

Borrowed
time
and
vessel

Letting the
magic
out

From
the inside
out

ENERGY SHIFT

Even my lip
is vibrating
pressure
points
draw tears

Labored
breath –
the currency
we gauge

Energy shift

I want
to grab
it
chase
it

And
bring it
back

That's
not
how
it
works

That's
not
how
it
works

Patricia Russo

Dream With Care

Dream
with
care

Be
discerning

Like
a sift
made
of love

Light
moves
the
pieces
through

Look
at
the stuff
that
sticks

What
does
your
heart
say

RUSTY

He wears
a
gold cross
on his
heart

And speaks
God's
language
"only as
he knows
God"

A silver
cross
sparkles
as it
hangs
from
her ankle

Surrounded

Tears
stream
as I
watch
her mini
tend
to her –
big
brown
eyes
of
innocence
and
hope

Wanting
approval

Bhakti
happens
here

In us
through us
out of us

Bhakti
happens
here

Hot Hips

Cold fingers
hot hips
hungry
lips

Open
heart

We move
friends
lovers

Stopping
time
by
the
candle's
light

Sexy
tunes
guide
us

Heart
wide
open
meeting
yours

Arjuna

Arjuna
in my
heart

I rap –
fingers
pads
palm

All tips
corners
and
creases
dance

Making
sense
beautiful
fierce
sense

Of the
cacophony
of
the Universe

In my
warrior's
song

Sexy
low
heartbeat
rhythm
from
layers
of lives
past

To the
surface
I call it

And add it
to the
vibration
that
is me

Foreplay

Our
foreplay
comes
in
soft
easy
syllables

You
see
me

We
push
pause
and
dance

Our
language
common,
sans
rules –
real

I
crave
it

Hungry

I watch
your lips
move

Hungry
for
each
phoneme

Your heart
here
at the
table
with us

Your eyes
thoughtful,
they
see me

And I
want
to cry
it feels
so
good

This love –
bottling
it up
to
drink it
at will

YOU

You –
my
hanky
panky

Ocean
window
eyes
I drown

Eager
lips
spill
love

Hands
velvet
hands
with
stories
to tell

My man
behind
closed
lids

Breathe
me
in

Warriors

They
line
the room –
warriors

And
we breathe
the
ocean's
breath

Together

Big gulps
and
slow sips

And move
as
one

I invite
the army
of
souls
I have
the honor
of
leading

To practice
from
the inside
out

Coins

I count
the days
and months
and
minutes
like coins
collected
polished

Breaths
and mala
beads

New skin
healed
heart

Whole
alone
happy

Gossamer Kisses

Wrap me
like lace

Cover me
with
transparent
wonder
tease me
diaphanously

Gossamer
kisses
on my
skin

Painted on
courage
covers
my delicate
parts
and
brave ones
too

Blue Checks

I watch
for
blue checks

And
listen for
the
chimes

Bringing
you
closer
to me

Blue bows
tied
neatly
kind eyes
lips
saying
my name

All of it
us
here
now
for
the taking

DETOUR

I lose
my head
with you

Fall back
into
a familiar
space

A detour
pause
steps away
from
the edge

High
numb
floating
fixed
matrix style
frozen

I examine
the frame
every
raw edge
I see me
there

Push play
and pull
her back
with
a sweet
kiss
and
a squeeze

Together
we are

We are

Sacred Geometry

We weave
in and out
of our
sacred
geometry

Time travelers
makers
and keepers
of magic

Ours
like honey

Sipping truth
and
making love –
with words
and
thoughts

Doers
lovers
plaid legs
fancy kicks –
with
many miles
to walk

BEACON

My hips
a beacon
calling

Your light
the
answer

You take
me in
with
both hands
and
open eyes

Breath

The gate
of
vulnerability
swings
open

We
walk
in

Broken Rule

Broke
a rule
just now
in the
game
of
silly

Why
do we
pretend
so
much

And
dance
or not

Around
the
subject
of
being

Really
in it —
eye contact
honest
real

I can
play
along
but
it's
a waste
of
time

Heavy Minutes

Heavy
minutes

Placing bets
with
myself

All in
against
my gut
as intuition
sits down
for
a chat

Full
dance card
options
pining
for
elusive
once
again

Checking
myself

Rolling up
the reel
saving
me
for
me

I Don't Know

I don't know
if
I have enough
love
for me

It sounds
like
a dreamy
idea
in theory

Right smack
in the
middle
of my bed

I want
for
nothing

Heart full
and wide
open

The love jar
lid off,
has
room —
lots

And…
I may not
have enough
to
fill it

MARTYR

Martyr
I choose
martyr

That way
I control
the dosage
of pain
one drop
in
at a time

And some
days
I turn
the
faucet
on
full blast

I feel
it
taking
me down
and laugh

"That's all you got?"
I ask –
hit me
with more
take me
to
the bottom
again

I know
that
place

And the map
to
crawl out

I See You

I see you —
Venice
in your
eyes

The ocean
waves
in your
hair

I want
to swim
there
frolic
be
create
whisper
and
shout

Instead
we
brunch
and
adopt
vintage
kicks

Your jar
is full
until
the
next
time

Magic In A Jar

Catching magic
in a jar

Savoring
sips
of
watermelon

Purple
handys
and
street kids

Vintage
kicks
and
soul-kissed
brunch

I frolic
in
the
magic
swimming
hole
of this
place

Fairy dust
on
my breath
and
street art
on
my skin

Mused
heart

I slip out
shimmy off
and drop
back in

Story Book Moon

Hanging
my hopes
on a storybook
moon
pinned
in an eternity
blue
sky

Lapsley
lullaby
Suptah
comfort
flannel
sheets
"Nice job PB,
I'll take it from here…"
Sixteen Candles
style
Goyte truth

Courage
falls short

Love
falls short

Truth
falls short

Here
in the depth
of me
paused
frozen

Sometimes
nothing
makes
sense

Nothing

But
the claps
and the
breaths
and the
heartbeats
measuring
time

Head
spinning
time

Empty

It's the
empty
feeling
the next
day
that
gets me

Cause
for pause
breath
yoga

RSVPing
yes
to the
invitation
today

Divine lover
let's
dance

To a
slow
sexy
heartbeat
tune

Bringing
me back
to whole
again

GREEN LIGHT

Take
the green
light
Universe
gift
and go

Parade
in
slow
motion
ego
on blast

Hell no's
define
hell yeses

Contrast
is
magic's
law

I look
through
the
ghosts
in
the
front
seats

And
roll
on

OUT OF BOUNDS

The
Old Fashion
takes
I'm
out of
bounds

Suddenly
craving
a pin cushion
body

Heart
what
heart

Intuition
hush

Numb
frozen
suspended
in time

10:09
the
lonely
hour

Goddess eyes
surround
me

Suptah
Baddha
Konasana

Shri Krishna
salty tears
and
deep breaths

Mission Grit

Mission grit
used passion
on the stoop

We create
together
as folks
pass

Whiskey
keeps me
honest

The light —
magic

Sophie B Hawkins
in my ear
heart
far away

Nothing matters

Nothing

Numb
mused
happy

11:11

Making a wish
of true love
to the glow
of 11:11
in the darkness

Playing hard
to get
talk
takes me
back

To a full
moon
in a different
sky

Fire sparks
fading over a
valley
of darkness

Foreshadowing

Give
the set designer
a raise

Games
not wished
or played

Only heart talk
welcome
here

IRONY

I read
a quote
today
about
the safety
in pain

And it
shook
me

Still making
my bed
with
its covers

Not quite
ready yet

Last ditch
numbing
to avoid
what's
real

Oh the irony

Her Glow

Her glow
across
the cardboard
paper
ridge

Soft
sexy
harmonious
ombre

The
magic
hour

Everything
dipped
in gold
flaws
erased –
silk

I glide
on 5
blonde tresses
tossed
by
her breath

Sunburn
tingle
reminding me
it was real

Ayn Rand Style

I watch you
Ayn Rand Style
and yawn

More proof
contrast
to vibrate
at a higher
frequency

Always pushed
by mimics

You're Gonna Die
on my
mind

Venice
in my
heart

Leaving
the hum
behind

Leaving
the hum
behind

La Ritournelle

Peeling back
the layers
with
La Ritournelle

Lover
layers

Healed
to arrive
in a new
place

With a
familiar tune
pulling
tugging
at the
soft openings
flapping
fleshy
vulnerable
pieces
of
my heart

The haze
has cleared
to leave
new pain
of clarity

Quiet
still
alone
in the
delicious
and terrifying
darkness
of me

Patricia Russo

Chemistry

The chemistry
is off

Solo orbit
in
pitch black
forever
darkness

Sipping truth
muddled
and cubed

Pondering
a snuffed
flicker

Her hands
keep me
here

And thoughts
of your
shadow
dancing
on the wall
beside
me

SOMETIMES

Sometimes
I want
to wave
the white
flag

Flip the switch
like he did

Start over

But
I know
better

It's not
a fresh
start
but a
loop
a silly
loop
where nothing –
nothing
is real

Except the
scars
the deep
scars

Stuck
on
repeat

Badass Motherfucker

Born of
intention
my
badass
motherfucker

Many
moons worth
of wait

Not from
here
a reminder
of bigger
things

Swimming
in the
lazy Sunday
light

Sheets bless us
sexy tunes
and nowhere
to be

Pinching
myself

Weaning Myself

Weaning myself
from unavailable

Putting the
sexy pics
in a box

I want
too

Give me
pieces
of you

Make yourself
mine
with no excuse
or care

Brave boy —
come
to me

I Love The Way

I love the way
your thumb
presses
into the heart
of my palm

Your boyish
eyes
speaking
to mine

How your lips
hunger
for honesty

Your tongue
speaking
far away
truth

The way
we move
together
without
moving
at all

How proud
you are
to
call me yours

LOVE WINS

Love wins
after
heartbreak
and a
toss

It wins
if it
ever
was

Love wins
in fleeting
moments
and
lasting
ones

In BC
crushes
and Tinder
words
fast Snaps
and
booty calls

Love wins
when you
choose

In all
shapes
and sizes
in seconds
and
in years

Love
wins

Forever Darkness

In
the
forever
darkness
of me
I
swim

Breathing
the stars —
cosmic
Prana

Unending
Seamless
Easy

My
liquid
soul

Satisfied

Belly full
of
an
essence
all mine —
only mine

Inhale
"I"
exhale
"Am"

Love

SIRENS

The Sirens
are singing
a low
tempo
melody
that cotton
can't even
quiet

They conspire
with my
muses
as the Universe
choreographs
every note

Goddesses

A fierce force
of energy
and light

A collective –
spinning
so fast
around me
that I am
lifted

Floating

At
their
every whim

Permission
granted
with an
open heart
and the
constant
oozing
of
letting go

Infrared Lens

I see
with
an infrared
lens

My pupils
and
pulse
sifting
collecting
searching
longing –
for
like energy

Vibration
Currency
Love

These bodies
matter
not

Limiting
vessels
and reminders
of
humanness

Ether
is
my Prana

Breathing
you in
one
delicious
atom
of brilliant
pulsing
humming
throbbing
particle
of essence
at
a time

CALLED TO COURT

Our souls
called
to court

Spirit
to
spirit
with only
one
law

Honesty

We stand
gazing
and I plead
for
my heart

Watching
with
clear intent
as you
show me
yours

For better
or
worse

Spring Is

Spring is
Paris
on
your lips

So
hungry
so
delicious

French kisses
that
stop
the world
around
you

Passion
that
ravishes
you

And
gently
oh so
gently
nudges
you
into
the
sweet spot

of
your
spinning
vortex

Take me

I am
yours

Take me

FRENCH

French
rolls
off his
tongue
and
billows
in a slow
sexy
smoky
dance

Carefully
slipping
its
grace-filled
tentacles
one
finger
at a time
from
my belly
to
my lips

His
words
my words

Wrap
us

Ravish
us

Fill
us

Meditation Pool

Swimming
Deliciously
for months
in the
meditation pool
of
my life

Happy
healed –
solo

Now:
standing
beside the pool
looking
into its
reflection
I dip my toe in
and I see
the friendly
ripple

Always
pulling me in

Today
I want to
share this water
open up

splash
float
and, and, and…

Paused
Frozen
suddenly

The ripple waits
my heart beats
the voice inside
says "go…"

I reach
my hand
out
for yours

I take a deep
deep
breath

And hope
without
fear
that you will
take it
and
swim
with me

COVERED

You cover
the canvas
of my skin
in kisses

Washed
from head
to toes

Bravely
I am there

Open

And wanting
of it
you
us

This time
that is not
and so
long
coming –
disappears
as suddenly
as it came

And
I work
to
shake
it off

In a Daze

We dance
a sexy
dance
of
one
in
a
cozy
single-room
squat
atop
the
city

You
take

I
take

In
a
daze
with
you
on
my skin

SHARED BREATH

Shared breath
and skin

Clouds
of
Krishna blue

A slow
melodic
heartbeat
chant
rings
in my
belly
and
beyond

With grace
and love
and care
you
take
my hand
in yours

And
so
it
is

SPIRITS

I wonder
when
our spirits
enter
this vessel
is it
suddenly?

Our choice
with seed –

Or with
the
first breath?

Do we
zero in
on a mama
and
a papa –
and jump
right in?

Or
slip in
with
an
inhale
as life
begins?

Dust

Your favorite
color
in dust

Proof
of a hold
not your
own

Your oui
a "way" —
of sorts

My heart
my guide

A map
so clear

My favorite
color
is love

Sober
Breathing
Yoga

I feel it all

I feel it all

FLUSHED

Flushed
A restart

Emptied
of
brightness

Dulled
to
the
bone

For what?

Contrast

Love
on
my
lips

Stars
on
the
moons
in
my
eyes

So that
I could
see
the
love
in you

It
pierced
me

Rash
Fleeting

A
sober
reminder

Noted

PAINTED GOLD

I watched
Paris
wake up

All of
her
awake
parts
painted
gold

The
sleepy
parts
lazy
with shade

Blue jay
bombers
dive
into
divine space

Quiet souls
keep
boxwood
and remove
yesterday
from
the cobbles

She wakes
with a
humble pace

New

Toss

Let
the Universe
toss
you
around
a bit

A
crescendo
building
suspense

Diamonds
pinned
in
a
black
velvet
sky

For
you
to
wear
like
cushion
pins

Or
doll

feelings
pierced
at
Her
whim

Held
in
the
palm
of
Her
hand

SARCELLE

She came
to us
by moonlight

Her full moon
energy
washed over us

The sarcelle
waters
in and out
in and out
with the tide

She held on
with
all of her
might

Until I
not so kindly
asked her
to go

LAST LIFE

Last life
words

Old soul
thoughts

Penned
prose

Verse
that comes
like the wind

Muses
Bubbles

Backdrops
of humanness

Fading vessel
Thirsty heart

Love
on
my
lips

You

You again

Home

Again

I said
I'd do it
again
and again

Despite
the
paralyzing
pain

And
here
I am

Hard-headed
Soft-hearted

Still
broken

Maybe always

It's not
about
this life
now

Brave
and
steady

footing
for
the
next one

I begin
again

Balanced Atoms

Balanced
atoms

Joined
and then
not

Fences

Jumping
Vaulting

Sonatas
one after
another

With steady
happy
pace

And then
four –

Haydn's
Surprise

Pause

Heart beats
Fear
Samskara

Over
and in
a tank

Not real
A rondo

Hands up

Hands in
prayer

Hands
on my heart

On
my knees

Tears
to
the sky

I begin
again

Glass Houses

From
a row
of
glass
houses

Perched
on
a
golden
thrown

Tossed
stones –
land
on
velvet
in
the
palm
of
my hand

I
glance
down

Wrap
my
fingers

one-by-one
around
the
shiny
pebbles
of projection

Smile
my heart
at
the tosser

And
walk
on

Just Know

Just know that
while you play
with truth
the way a cat plays
with a defenseless mouse
I pursue
more serious options

Just know that
while you dance
with shadows
on the wall
I'm in my skin
dancing with lovers

Just know that
the far away
romance you represent
is really my fantasy –

Manifested
from ash

Penned
by heart

Breathed
in and out
in a slow, mindful
cadence

Scripted
Crafted
Rehearsed

Until I say, "Cut!"

Just know
It is mine

Just know

Pulse

I have
my finger
on
the pulse
as She
beats
so
do I

Pulling
directly
from Source
a conduit
for
working
Her magic

I pull
the breath
in
adding me
and exhale
used

It comes
swiftly
not mine
to keep
but rather
to make
share

and
let go

And so it is

Heaven Spot

From your
Heaven Spot

Spent
toonies
rare
(and strange)
like paper
here

Faith

Bold greed
on the take

My heart
on
a string
a Pay Stub
brushed
on
with glue
temporary

Not yours
not mine –

Hers

Ripple Effect

I dip my toe
just past
the plane
of glassy
reflection
and watch
the ripple –
effect

A circle
within circles

Bored with most
he says
with boyish
man eyes
and words
from another
place

Verbose
beyond
his years
yet stuck

A reminder
of this journey
within
and without

Riddled
with
torments

10 BEADS

10 beads
I count
like
108
precious
stones
tied
together

And I pause

Guru
Gopa
God
Divinity

I see
in the eyes
of each
soul sent
and met
on this
path

Sipping power
eating courage

Work
Play
Read
Heal

It is written
in the book
of blessings

A creed sealed
with a reminder
on the sundial
in a silent
courtyard
that holds
many secrets

SEDUCED

Seduced
with
each pull
like breath
drinking
me in
and adding
my drops
to
the whole

The smell
of morning
and Her magic
on
my arm

Reminded
of power
given
and taken

Finding
a new
Zen

Parallel Universes

I float
in and out
of
parallel
universes

Warrior heart
in hand
as if
it lives
outside of
my body

All of this
moot

This is not real

Constantly
aiming my arrow
at my
soul pursuit

Limited
at times
by this
human body

Her Hair

Her hair
was like
a
White Snake
Video

Sunset cruises
Michelada
chats
about
free love

The kind
I crave

My heart
isn't
as brave
as the
rest
of me

It wants
to ask
for
what
it wants

Numbed
by red

Living
for
Tuesday

I want you
and
I don't know
how to ask

On Juniper

In my dream
we lay there
hand in hand
on Juniper
in the meadow
of pine
the warm
earth
below us

A day's worth
of living
in our shoes

The galaxy of
stars breathing
above us

Dippers we can touch
diamonds pinned
in vast velvet
surrounding us

And for a moment
nothing else
matters

But your hand in mine

Your hand
in mine

YOUR BREATH

Your breath
comes
in waves
on my
island
shoulder

Your pulse
between
my fingers –
life

The sleep in
saves me

A pause
frozen
in my
mind reel

I catch
one beat
and
hold it
with
all
my might

Until
the
next
time

Packed

Packed
lotus seeds
in leather

A toonie
on the
stand

I smell
you
here
with me

Among
the lingering
memory
of "us"

"Let"
and "go"
on my
breath

ALGIZ

Algiz arrow
the divine might
of the Universe
my protection

Sacred
set apart
from mundane
blessed

I garner
courage
and face
fear
head on

Acting
in spite
of fear
and not
because

Feathers
and arrows
at my feet
carry me
along

Crash Into Me

Crash
on the radio
takes me back
to a time
of young love —
college love

The fear
of providing
was nonexistent
and your big hand
held mine

Our life in front of us
a big map
lots of time
hiked up skirts
worlds
lessons —
lots of lessons

Foolish
to think
it could be
different

10 years pass
what lessons
have I learned

I look in the mirror
and I see wrinkles
a girl
with time
on her face
and love
in her core

With a heart
that is molded
by lovers' hands
into the woman
that she is now

Ask

Ask for
what you
want

Do it
with
fierce grace

Break yourself
wide open
and let
the light
pour in

Covering
every part
sealed
and
dripping
extra
drops

That magnetically
attach
to like
souls
and
energy

Connecting you
forever

Cast
with a
rune
of protection
on an
old bridge
by
the light
of
a blue moon

SOMEHOW

Somehow
in that moment
the power
I gave you
was yours

To take
spin
swallow
chew
spit out —
kiss

Grab…

Like a cherished
breath
one that you
aren't sure
will return

You breathed
it in
mine
and yours
and let it all go

SHADE

That shade
you cast
is respite
for my
fire

Transparent
stoking
that I take
in
with a big breath
filtered
pranayama

I add
love
before
sending it back
out

I breathe fire
the cleansing
kind

And your
soul kindling
will not
go
to waste

Into the fire
we go

As one

DREAMING

Dreaming of
"what can I
do for you"

Drinking up
"proud
of you"

Words
are
gold

Easy
currency

Empty
your till

Feel it
be it
say it

By the River

Spend
the weekend
with me
by the river
under
the stars
like teenagers
time
matters not

The difference
a year
makes

Silly girl –
intuition dodger
unavailable bait
is your
poison

Dance
with that
kryptonite
in your hand
dance

Spin
recklessly

I'm here
when
you are ready
to listen

A gift
I will give
to your
heart

A gift
I will give
to your soul

A gift
I will give

Fading Pixels

It's not real

Fading
pixels

Snapped
with
false courage

Masked
unavailable
safe

Stuck on repeat
an old pattern

Cupcakes and bubbles
bed bounces
and brunch

Hiding in the
nothingness

Echoes of "Oh boy"
days past
courage on the table
staring into
the Sakshat
mirror

A finger tap
is all
it takes
for the
water
to rush out
and a big
gulp
to
rush in

Paper House

I'm building
a paper
house
on
the beach

And I'm
summoning
Her fierce
breath

With all
the
magic
I can
conjure

No looking
back
only
steps forward

Dragon wings
flapping
cliffs below

Wealth
piled up
all around
me

Deserving
so deserving
of the
vortex swirls
and
mind blowing
Devo Maheshwara

And so it is

And so it is

TEARS

For a long time
the tears
ran like
a faucet
abundant
and fierce
full of emotion

Today they come
like stars
in the Tahoe night
brilliant
solid
glistening
with a powerful
tug

I want to
tether myself
to them
and scream
"Hit it!"
and ride
solemn
through
the night
sky

Reckless
brave
fierce
life on fire

Diamonds
on my
cheeks

Matrix Style

In the car
one year later
Matrix style
paused
only the sound
of
deep
slow
melodic
breaths
grounded
listening

Play –
fireworks
certainty
without fear
or abandonment
certainty
guided by
lives past
and future
days too

Now

Stop the car
get out
what's mine is mine
what's yours is yours

In an instant
past walls crumble

with the cutting
of the cord
a new Now
is created

I feel it all

I am it all

I watch
eyes and heart
wide open
as the grid
is rewired
new DNA
is written
and applied
paradigms
realities
divinity
sacred geometry
appears
and I
touch it

I breathe
it in

Home

I am home

SHREDDING

My heart
shreds
in a new
way
these days

On a
dirt path
to nowhere
and everywhere
at once

Drishti lessons
I wear –
painful reminders
of a
different sort

Playing

Being

Following
courage

Sweet Soft Intention

I wanted to
touch you,
instead
I watched
carefully
as your eyes
told me
everything

Lips speaking
sweet
soft intention
to
mine

Time is
a slow
dance –
our dance
and I
like it

Truth Dancers

Truth dancers
dance
with me
fire
in our
bellies

No permission
to
ask for
giving notice

Our time
is now

We dance
with
divine purpose
courage
real intuition –
love

Kindling –
our fires
catch

We are
contagious

We are
ripples

We are
one

Dance
with me

I Notice

I notice
the happy
and
not-so-happy
lines

The wrinkles
and creases

Each
with a story
to tell

Of this
crazy beautiful
life
in a body
marked
by time
lived by
heart
and driven
by love

From The Stars

Boyish eyes
and a first,
do you come from
the stars too?

I recognize
light
and feel it

Here,
beside me
gazing
intrigued

And far away
heart flips
too

Navigating
these waters
swimming
in velvet

Dear Hell Yes

Dear Hell Yes
with a tambourine

I'm
not really
that scary

Paddle
into
your fear
holding your breath
when the wave
takes you

I promise
you'll be okay

SPIDERS

I saw
your eyes
today —
while
the spiders
did
their work

Seared
onto
the grid

Powerful
needles
of medicine
when
plugged
into
this light

Reminds me
that
I AM

SIFTER

Turn offs
and
turn ons

Coarse
character bits –
left
in the
sifter

Medicine
homework
breadcrumbs

Relics

Tiny
dream catchers
and
a Ganesha –
relics
on the dash
of
my life

Catching
and
removing

Catching
and
removing

WORKS IN PROGRESS

Crazy
and messy
but
I love it

Choice,
she wants
to dance

Twisted
in all
the right ways

We're a
thousand miles
from comfort

Works in progress

Little Red Corvette

Little Red Corvette
your way
takes me back
to that Chicago night
and the deep
part of me
is touched,
again

Sexual healing
personified
by a magic maker
with real deep eyes
and power
harnessed
and directed
with intention –

I observe
and want it

Good-bye beautiful
2014
you've given me
the gift
of me
a melody my own
so strong,

courage and power
wrapped
in an unbreakable
container

An unbreakable
container

Up With The Sun

Up with the sun
making art
with this body
of mine

Light kisses
on my skin
hairs on end
cold earth
beneath me

Surrounded
by a vastness
that
swallows me up

And I let it

My People

My people
blood
land
native

In a circle
of souls
I sit —
and cry
as the carved
wood
melody
stirs my blood
mixed instantly
with theirs,
recognition

Innate proof
that we are one
and that
experience
is far beyond
this lifetime

Drawn to
this place
again
my toes
on sacred earth,
roots —
my heart
is theirs

HANGED FOOL

A Hanged Fool
reality
truth
from a different
perspective

Not everyone
sees
the stars
upside down
where the ocean
should be

I breathe
from the bottom
to the top

Balanced on
poet's
feet

Heart wrapped
in bandha
wrapped in
time –
time that flies

BELL

There's a bell in my hand
but I don't feel it

And so it is
brings me back
into my body
with a tear

Figure eights
in needles
on my ankles

Silver cord connection
navigating
the pink and blue
with breath

Rose wax and fresh earth
ooze and drift in
grabbing hold
and signaling home

I float above
and watch

I could fly anywhere
making promises
with the moon

Fine Line

There's
a fine
line
between
brilliance
and
madness —
I love
watching
you
walk it

About The Author

Sometimes, when we're lucky, life allows us to actually meet someone whose being truly inspires us. And sometimes, if we're really lucky, that person becomes a part of our lives and uses their light to illuminate potential we were never able to see in ourselves. And sometimes, if we're really, really lucky, that person becomes a North Star, a constant despite the space created by the changes in life, always with us. That person, for me, is Patricia Russo.

Pat and I met when we were young teachers, trying to make the world a better place one student at a time. At first I found it hard to believe that a person could be so smart, talented, creative, beautiful, loving, and kind, but she is, and in the most genuine and real way possible. As colleagues we shared ideas and laughs; as friends we shared dreams and tears. Pat became one of the biggest cheerleaders I've ever had in my life. She was the first of us to take a leap into a new career path, once again inspiring me and showing me the magic possible when you trust in your own wings.

I hope you have the luck to meet Pat in person, but if nothing else, after reading her book you will know her. You will know her light and her love, and you must know that it is true. All of it. She is rare, and she is beautiful, and she is constant. And I am all the better for knowing and loving her back.

Made in the USA
Middletown, DE
11 January 2017